The Break Dance Kids

Poems of Sport, Motion, and Locomotion

The Break Dance Kids
Poems of Sport, Motion, and Locomotion
by Lillian Morrison

LOTHROP, LEE & SHEPARD BOOKS   NEW YORK

Library of Congress Cataloging in Publication Data
Morrison, Lillian.
  The break dance kids.
  Summary: A collection of poems about sports,
dancing, and other physical activities.
  1. Children's poetry, American. 2. Sports—
Juvenile poetry. 3. Dancing—Juvenile
poetry. 4. Motion—Juvenile poetry. [1.
American poetry. 2. Sports—Poetry. 3.
Dancing—Poetry. 4. Motion—Poetry] I. Title.
PS3563.08747B7 1985   811′.54
  84-23396
ISBN 0-668-04553-7   ISBN 0-668-04554-5 (lib. bdg.)

Acknowledgments

Some of the poems appeared first in the following publications: "Ernie" in *The Ghosts of Jersey City*, copyright © 1967 by Lillian Morrison; "Morning Ringside" in *Urthkin*; "Kumina" as "Kumina, Jamaica" in *Glassworks*; "The A Train" in *Miranda's Music* by Jean Boudin and Lillian Morrison, copyright © 1968 by Lillian Morrison; "Dark Eyes at Wimbledon" as "Dark Eyes at Forest Hills" in the anthology *Sprints and Distances*, copyright © 1965 by Lillian Morrison; "Downhill Racer" in the anthology *Atalanta*, copyright © 1984 by Papier-Maché Press; "Just for One Day" in the anthology *The Random House Book of Poetry for Children*, copyright © 1983 by Random House, Inc.

The photographs on pages 13, 16–17, 26, 32, 38–39, 50, 54–55, and 60 are winners of the Scholastic Photography Awards, conducted by Scholastic Magazines and sponsored by the Eastman Kodak Company. The photographers and the year of their award are: p. 13, Brian Brainerd, 1976; pp. 16–17, Timothy Pott, 1980; p. 26, unknown, 1975; p. 32, David Wessel, 1969; pp. 38–39, Peter Byrne, 1973; p. 50, Tom Houghton, 1964; pp. 54–55, Ted Anastas, 1975; p. 60, Christopher Lewis, 1979. The author wishes to express appreciation to Eudora M. Groh of Scholastic, Inc., for making these photographs available.

The author also thanks the following for the use of their photographs: Jacket, title page, and page 10, Martha Cooper; pp. 20 and 48, M. De Chiara; p. 24, Henry Chalfant; pp. 30–31, Mookie, Hubie, and Strawberry and the New York Mets; pp. 36–37 and 62, Bettye Lane; p. 42, Stella Snead; p. 45, Sara Lupton Jennings, p. 53, AP/Wide World Photos.

For Esther Jean, aerobic dancer and athletic gardener
and
For Phil, who long ago predicted
I would write poems about sport

Contents

B Boy

As onlookers clap
and rap and shout
I curl up and turn myself
inside out.

I can jig horizontal
as I lean on one hand;
I'm a spin-top, a pinwheel,
a one-man dance band,

inventing new moves
when I get a notion.
I can take out the best.
I'm graffiti in motion,

a sidewalk tornado
to the rhythm of rock.
Meet the baddest break dancer
(that's me) on the block.

Basketball Players

"It's possible for a player
to jump because he's happy,
but it's more likely that he's
happy because he's jumping."
—Bill Russell in *Second Wind*

When we're happy,
we jump for joy.
Basketball players
jump as ploy
to get the ball
or net the ball.
Jump! Slamdunk!
Come down, splatSPLAT.
They get *their* joy
out of that.
And they like the sound,
as well as the soaring,
as they pound down the floor,
of the crowd roaring.

When I Read

I'm a runner, a racer,
I've got a lot of speed.
I can sprint
from here to   there
with time to spare.
But when I *read*
then I'm a diver!
I plunge
        right
                in
and until the story's over
I don't come up for air.
Then too I'm an explorer,
a tracker and a rover
and I always
find something
I didn't know was there.

SPORT
portside
sideline
lineback
backhand
handball
ball game
game, set
set, match
match play
playground
ground rule
rule book
BOOK

The 100 Meters

Sprung from the starting blocks
they punch down the stretch
fly   gulp air as the stride
quickens as arms flail try
try   the agonized moment
drops.

Beyond the finish line
they jog a little,
bend over, saunter off,
the winner's arm round the neck
of a glad supporter.

Later, hands on hips,
those springing limbs
now leaning at ease,
they rest on the laurels
of noble exertion
and listen for the time.

Ernie

He used to box.
He was no ox.
Among the shills,
He was the fox.

Slim, tricky, neat,
Quick on his feet,
He was the prince
Of Quincy Street.

I liked his stance.
He did his dance.
He'd take on any
Bout with chance.

But chance's whim
Outpointed him
And one day took him
Limb by limb.

Morning Ringside

The top of the tulip tree
boxes with the wind,
bobs, weaves, tips way over
(that roundhouse really landed)
and the birds whistle,
scream for a knockout
loud enough to lift me,
knocked out all night,
onto my feet again
before the count of ten.

Two to Nothing

Catcher, the ball caller
  knees bent, squatting;
Pitcher, a slider guider
  peering, plotting.
First up, a pop up
  hung his head, spit.
Next up, a bloop looper
  got a cheap hit.
Then came a bunt dumper
  out at first base
  (a runner with pep
  but out by a step).
Then came the power,
  the big number one
slammed a low pitch
  for a towering home run.

Water Incident

We chug-chug out to the island
in our bicycle boat,
the little dog, our figurehead,
pointing the way.
Eager but unreliable
our figurehead jumps in the lake.
We have to pull her out.
She wets us with her spray.

the swimmer

enters
the sheets
    swims
into position
stretches
      floats
into a slow
    somersault

backwards
  overeasy

(ah, cool ocean)
stretches again
legs e
   l
    o
     n
  to s g
    t   a
    r   t
     e   e
      a   d
       m
        e
         r
          s
exhaustion
  flowing out
    through toes
      and fingertips

sleeps

23

Electric Boogie

Now I do the moon walk,
Watch my feet,
Heel, toe, backward glide,
Right to the beat.
I'm walking in space, man.
I am the ace, man.

How We Dance

Jimmy dances like a jittery mannekin,
Debbie like a limp rag doll,
Heather like an ocean wave with deep undulation,
Betty like a bird in thrall.
Charles dances like a benevolent serpent,
Bonnie like a beach ball floating on the sea,
Steve like a volcano, all sudden smooth eruptions,
Penny like a pendulum that suddenly has conniptions.

Kumina

(Ritual dance: Kingston, Jamaica)

I tap on it
till the hummin' comin'
said the drummer
and the hum comes
and the thunder
and the blood drums
as the god's black queen
a spider bee
steps regally
to high stinging cries
of singing
and the dancers fly
out of their bodies.

The A Train

I sail home on crescendos
Straphanging, scale home
on wailing rails and shrilling whistles.
Look, man, one hand!
Now skate along smooth grates
Rockety   rocking   faster
Swacketing down the track
(O shrieking screamer streaming down)
Held swinging in the growing dying roars.

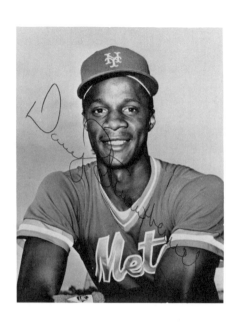

Again and Again

(The 1983 Season)

I switch the bedside radio off,
a faint ache in my legs and feet,
not to mention the heart, and try
to sleep but cannot. We had
the bases loaded in the ninth, two
out, the tying run at the plate.
Oh, why do they always do this
to me? We were only down by four!
But sweet Strawberry just struck out,
and the Mets have lost once more.

Let's Go, Mets

(Opening of the 1984 Season)

Mookie and Hubie and Strawberry,
These are the guys in the lineup for me.
Hernandez can hit, play first base with style,
Foster comes through every once in a while.
But for hustle and muscle and artistry,
Give me Mookie and Hubie and Strawberry.
These are my hopefuls, these are my three:
Mookie and Hubie and Strawberry.

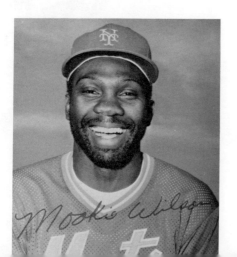

Bike Tour

Spray and early sun,
misty clean morning,
as row on row of flat
breakers roll in, and
a lone surfer rides them
in the white light of dawn.

We breathe deep and watch.
How good the oranges taste
before we mount our bikes
again, dawn behind us,
to take on noon and night,
pores open, head on.

The Speed Skaters

When the skaters push
with powerful thighs
round the rink
leaning far forward
streamlined for speed,
do they think,
"This may be thin ice?"
Oh no. Air is the
adversary, and time,
suits are skintight
the better for swimming
and their long arms
swing in great arcs.

Orangutans of grace
alien creatures
freed from normal laws
of human speed
they offer us the gift
of their slick
self-propelling.
Now, for the moment,
we too are swift
beyond barriers.

Park Action

The jogger runs under
the dome of trees
trots through air
hair flapping.

Speckled with light
full of talk
the ladies on benches
shake heads at each other.

Branches sway
bristling with leaves
pigeons strut
peck, peck, pecking.

The sun shoots
through every opening
as suddenly wind-pushed
the runner sprints.

Runners

Time never gets tired.
Still there is the will
tempted always to test it,
tease it, overcome—
the marathoner, numb
with pain, suddenly weightless
treading on clouds,
the miler's kick on the gun lap,
the sprinter's burst
to come in first.

Photograph by Bettye Lane

May the hidden clocks
never show their wrinkled
faces to you, striders,
who run for us biders of time
and carry us, past
tenths of seconds,
to a survival   in purest air
where even time's no rival.

To an Olympic Hopeful
or
The Transcendentalist

for L. M. T.

By means of every race,
pacing, striding, pounding
through measured space,
prepared   for reaching
by jogging over hills,
you slowly move
toward that far, difficult
high place
we only look at

and simply
through joy in running

and the will to do,
with a rueful smile
at the blinking star
you've hitched your wagon to.

A fair-haired acolyte
in a plain but sacred rite,
may you always serve
in satisfaction
your self-imposed ideal
(which makes you real)
with faith, friends, and exercise
to uphold you
just as Emerson told you.

Gold Medalist

In all my endeavor
I wish to be ever
A straight arrow spearing
Just past the possible.

Dark Eyes at Wimbledon

He gazed at her with his whole soul.
His look contained his all.
For she was the nearest linesman
And he didn't like the call.

The Animal Kingdom

(With apologies to J. R. Crowley)

What football scatback
can score like a squirrel?
What diver match a dolphin?
Who can leap like a cat?

What gold medal runner
can ever catch a cheetah?
Who can swim like a mackerel
or fly like a bat?

The animal kingdom
has the best athletes.
What do you make of that?

Canoe and Ducks

In smooth single file
eight mergansers glide;
first in a circle
then in a row they
ride the water mirror.

Now they huddle,
now spread out, now
dip heads in the lake
without a splash;
then rise and shake
their feathers,
following the leader.

We watch the silent
aquacade. They
sail on one by one,
and, dipping paddles,
we glide as soundlessly,
the sun, now
dipping too and gone
below the horizon.

The Break Dance Kids
or
No More Gang Wars

No more gangs
              now they are crews
         who dance the news
               of the street
                  the Rock Steady Crew
            the Dynamic Breakers

    compete
           on the pavement
                in impossible feats
         of gyration
            to rhythm of rap
                to beat of hip hop

         like corkscrews
             they spin,
          on heads, backs, shoulders
            legs racing,
   then stop   in a freeze.

Maniac whirls
     into a hand glide
    Crazy Legs does his
        automaton's slide.

    Float like a zephyr
      slither   in waves
       like a snake
     rockit like a robot
       tick like a clock
     their fights
  are mock now   their fights
    are rock now
      Rock Steady.

Two Points

Ball,I'mgonnawashyou
in the shower of the
net *Whoosh!* you
gonna come
through
clean

Slalom Skier

Snow dancer
        slant dancer
                adept in the art
            of swivelling
    he tangoes down
through the tall stalks
        with their fluttering flags
                not one is missed
        then does the twist
            as the gates
                    come closer
            and closer together
                    smoothly angles
        in and out
                    threads each one
        until the final
            hissing glide
                and the run is done.

Downhill Racer

Over the snow-covered
slopes and dips she
swoops   flies   skis
sighing   skims bumps
and hollows   rounding
the turns to race the
reeling clock   zips
down   down   rocking
for the last speck
of speed   *uh-oh!*
almost tumbles   re-
covers   now hunched
  for the long
                schuss
                    in.

Did she win?
A hundredth of a second
could make the difference.
She smiles in spite of
fears   removes goggles.
The mountainsides
reverberate with cheers.

The Bicyclist

The possible paths unroll,
hills, curves, sheer straightaway
as down his strip of road
the bicyclist
pedals persistent
rides on within
the bubble of his intent
unaware that the world is round
and whirling.

The Old Pro

In that country long ago
there were houses
with magic windows
through which he sprang
as on to open fields
where anything might Be or Sing or Happen.
Bluebells leaned on beer cans,
rang their jingles in the clover,
fences did snake dances
sticks rattling them to rhythm
and balls flew far in climbing arcs
beneath a brand-new sun.

Now, with smoked windows,
trains from the hills arrive,
a little late. Teams debark
laden with luggage. They move slowly
past the low porches to the old field
with the half-filled bleachers
where each man waits his turn.

He walks to the plate,
takes his stance
smiling, though his legs hurt,
for his eye is sharp
and he's on home ground.
He can still meet the ball
and a familiar sun streams down
through the waning afternoon.

Attempted Steal

On the mound, the pitcher shook off
a sign, wound up, and threw.
On first, the runner took off;
the catcher's throw was true.
Runner in with a head-first slide,
Ball was faster than he reckoned.
It matters not how hard he tried.
He slid and did-and-died at second.

Sometimes They Get There

Unlike the turtle
Subways hurtle
Unless they stall
And don't move at all.

Just for One Day

Hey, sidewalk pacers
bumper riders
long-legged gliders
stalkers, ledge walkers
roof straddlers
fence jumpers
stompers, trouncers
muggers, sluggers
big burly bouncers
alley runners
stabbers, purse grabbers
hurriers, harriers
scared scurriers
all chased and chasers
please cease for a moment
oh please,
lie down in a heap
and sleep.

The Finish Line

There is the finish line
but the runner can cross it
again and again.

She will not be finished
for a long time
but always beginning

getting ready and set
for another GO!
a better finish.

Also by Lillian Morrison

Overheard in a Bubble Chamber
and Other Sciencepoems

The Sidewalk Racer
And Other Poems of Sports and Motion

Who Would Marry a Mineral?
Riddles, Runes & Love Tunes